30 DAYS
of HOPE

FOR PEACEFUL LIVING

GIFTS OF HOPE SERIES

The "Gifts of Hope" series is a collection of 30-day, short devotionals focused on various life issues and needs. Offering personalized Scripture selections and prayers that provide readers with inspiration and hope, these messages make wonderful gifts for the people in your life, who need encouragement.

Forthcoming topics in the "Gifts of Hope" series include:

ADOPTION

CHILD SICKNESS

CHRONIC ILLNESS

FINANCIAL STRUGGLE

HURTING MARRIAGES

INFERTILITY

SINGLENESS

WEARINESS

To learn more, visit **NewHopePublishers.com**

GIFTS OF HOPE SERIES

30 DAYS *of* HOPE

FOR PEACEFUL LIVING

MARK BETHEA

NEW HOPE®
PUBLISHERS
Gospel-Centered. Missions-Driven.
Birmingham, Alabama

New Hope® Publishers
PO Box 12065
Birmingham, AL 35202-2065
NewHopePublishers.com
New Hope Publishers is a division of WMU®.

Library of Congress Control Number: 2015940022

ISBN-10: 1-59669-437-8
ISBN-13: 978-1-59669-437-8

N154115 • 0715

ACKNOWLEDGMENTS

THANKS BE

To God, for His never-ending faithfulness and provision

To my chief encourager and friend, Brittany, and

To my parents, whose example I hope to follow.

TABLE OF CONTENTS

Introduction

• • •

Day 1

Acknowledgments

I would like to thank Andrea Mullins for asking me to write on peace for this distinctive devotional series from New Hope® Publishers. The process has allowed me great reflection—and clarity. I'm so appreciative of the entire New Hope team for helping and leading in this new endeavor. Thanks to Joyce Dinkins and Melissa Hall for your feedback, comments, and help in crafting these devotionals.

I'm so thankful for my faith family at Argo Baptist Church, Alabama. Thanks for your patience, love, support, and encouragement this past year.

And to my wife, Brittany, and all my family and friends: thank you for your prayers, presence, and encouraging words. I'm eternally grateful for each of you.

INTRODUCTION

If you are reading this devotional, you are not immune to times of great strife and pain. But I want to assure you, you are also able to receive peace that will pull you through. There is hope ahead. For the next 30 days, we will journey together to discover how we can receive a perfect peace from God, who willingly and lovingly embraces His own. Each day, we will review a passage of Scripture along with encouragement to connect us with God's heart. You can also find a Scripture index that lists helpful verses, to reflect on peace, hope, rest, and relief.

I began writing this devotional at a time when I desperately needed God's peace. It was something I never intentionally sought. I knew that in the chaos surrounding me, I needed something, but I couldn't quite grasp what experiencing a measure of God's peace looked like. I surely tried to manufacture peace by surrounding myself with tranquil and restful moments, but there was still restlessness in my spirit. The sort of restlessness that keeps you up deep into the night, night after night. My mind wandered to the fear of the unknown and instead of resting in the goodness of God, I laid awake, frozen in fear.

As my world seemed to crumble around me, I began to understand more and more how peace looks and feels.

· · · · ·

I vividly remember looking into my mother's eyes as we received the diagnosis that she had developed stage-four pancreatic cancer that had spread to numerous other places in her body. The doctor and his assistant slowly and carefully explained the ramifications of their findings to my dad, my brother, and me in the small, curtained-off room somewhere in the deep recesses of the hospital.

It was a moment in time that stood still. What took no more than 30 seconds for the doctor to deliver felt like an eternity as our world came crashing down with each passing word.

First, disbelief and the surreal nature of the news went wild in my mind. Next, chaos erupted. I couldn't focus or think until . . . I looked again into my mom's eyes.

Her eyes radiated a peace that surpassed my highest expectations.

How could she look like that? She had received a diagnosis numbering her remaining days of life. There was a sadness, but trumping her sadness was a determined and confident peace about what she had just heard.

When the doctors departed and we were left with our thoughts, we held hands and prayed together for God to grant us peace and wisdom going forward. But uppermost in my mind was what I saw my sweet mother's eyes demonstrating. Peace, from the heart of God straight through the pen of Paul: "And the peace of God, which surpasses all understanding, will guard your hearts and your minds in Christ Jesus" (Philippians 4:7). I wanted that.

I wanted to be filled with that sort of peace. And that day, I believe that, through the prayers of countless individuals, God did guard her heart and mind in Jesus with a peace that surpasses what should have been.

Yes, the diagnosis was bad.

Yes, we were all scared.

Yes, she understood the reality of the diagnosis.

But, peace reigned supreme over fear. It reigned over the future. It reigned and guarded our hearts and minds.

There's more to Philippians 4 than this one verse, and we'll take time to examine what comes before and what comes after, but this is our goal.

As I face each day, no matter the circumstance, I want to have the peace that my mother experienced that day. It was not something she created to face the doctor's words but was given wholly by God in our time of greatest need.

Whether we are in the midst of desperation and fear now or know we will go through this in the future, we must build foundations to prepare for the storms of life that will rage in our lives.

30 DAYS OF HOPE for Peaceful Living

DAY 2

REJOICE

"Rejoice in the Lord always; again I will say, rejoice."

—Philippians 4:4

• • • • •

. . . . .

During my first few weeks in my first pastorate, at Argo Baptist Church right outside of Birmingham, Alabama, our family received the report about Mom's cancer. I wrestled that week. What could I possibly say to my new church family? My heart was broken and my spirit beaten down. But somehow I was supposed to take to the pulpit and share about the goodness of the Lord and the glory of the gospel.

"Rejoice in the Lord always; again I will say, rejoice" (Philippians 4:4). This was the foundational Bible text for my preaching. *Rejoice in the Lord always. How? I don't think Paul could have possibly been referring to my situation. What is there to rejoice in, in this hurt?* Slowly, in frustration, and with great difficulty, I began to see how much there was and is to rejoice in.

In Christ, we have endless reasons to rejoice.

This is where we begin to shift our thinking. We can look at the evidence around us and begin to feel the gloom and despair of the situation, or we can choose to reflect on what God has done through Christ for us.

Understandably, each of us has so much we could focus on and even grumble about. There are sickness and disease, employment troubles, family troubles, brokenness, and so on. But, there is a truth that remains steady: God sent His beloved Son to earth to redeem and bring hope into the world.

If we stop to reflect on what God has done—not on our situations—we have endless cause for rejoicing.

There is ample reason for Paul to beckon us to rejoice— twice within one sentence. As I sat to prepare the sermon for that particular Sunday morning, I had to read and reread this simple sentence countless times. *Rejoice in the Lord always. Always rejoice in the Lord. Rejoice. Rejoice always.* Rejoicing is an intentional decision we make. The default mode we often live in is not a spirit of rejoicing, but we can choose to rejoice, understanding our present position with Christ, secure in our salvation.

Our salvation is secure in the Cross of Christ. It may be helpful for us to sit today and simply read, meditate, and memorize this short verse. Rejoicing isn't natural, and it surely isn't easy. But it is instrumental in finding and maintaining a peaceful spirit.

How can we let a temporary crisis block our rejoicing?

I am so thankful that God led me to preach through Philippians before my family knew what would happen to my mom. I don't find it coincidental that the text I would preach the week we learned of her illness would be these words from Philippians 4:4.

My circumstances forced me to dwell on the goodness of the Lord and to remind myself that I have endless reason to rejoice amidst any present reality. It's far too easy to look to what we see and to despair. But we must focus our gaze on what has been done already for us by Christ's redemption on the Cross.

DAY 3

THERE IS AN END

"Let your reasonableness be known to everyone. The Lord is at hand."

—Philippians 4:5

• • • • •

. . . . .

One of the most helpful things I was told during my difficulty was to remember the temporary nature of what we experience on earth. Paul reminds his readers that "the Lord is at hand." We know He is coming back, and we know that what we experience on earth pales in comparison to what we will experience in what is to come.

When I was young, I broke my arm twice, back-to-back. The first time I was in the backyard playing football, and soon thereafter, I ran straight into a door. The pain was intense, but the suffering had a tangible timeframe that I could understand. I had a hard, protective cast covering my arm, but I knew there would be a day when the itchy, scratchy, and annoying plaster would come off. As frustrating as it was to take showers with my arm wrapped in a trash bag, I knew this circumstance was not forever. The day was coming when the doctor would saw off the cast and my arm would be free and healed. We can have the same expectation of our trials.

Sickness, disease, hardships, frustrations, and every circumstance *will have an end.*

Everything is temporary. Everything we are struggling through right now will eventually end. Let this be good news to you today. We can enjoy and savor the good things we experience. And we can endure the difficulty, knowing that this too shall pass.

So we do not lose heart. Though our outer self is wasting away, our inner self is being renewed day by day. For this light momentary affliction is preparing for us an eternal weight of glory beyond all comparison, as we look not to the things that are seen but to the things that are unseen. For the things that are seen are transient, but the things that are unseen are eternal.

—2 Corinthians 4:16–18

Dwell on that which we cannot see, on what is coming. In our greatest struggle, the more we sit on the strife, the more we lose focus of the reality of eternity—the promised hope by which we can continue. Paul urges us to press forward and not to lose hope. Even though conditions may deteriorate, we are closer to the day when all will be made new.

The writers of the New Testament often repeated the idea that the Lord is at hand and that Christ is coming back soon, reminding us to focus on eternity in light of earthly pulls and pressures.

What you see before you today will pass. But the things that are most precious, namely your salvation and the love of God in Christ Jesus, are eternal.

Your salvation in Christ doesn't come and go. It is secure. You will remain in the love of God through Christ long after your momentary, earthly affliction fades into history.

DAY 4
OVERWHELMING ANXIETY

"Do not be anxious about anything, *but in everything by prayer and supplication with thanksgiving let your requests be made known to God.*"

—Philippians 4:6, author's emphasis

•   •   •   •   •

• • • • •

This may be one of most difficult passages in all of Scripture to apply. "Do not be anxious about anything." Look closely. Paul does not implore us to not be anxious about most things but reminds us to not be anxious about *anything*.

In other words, there is no single thing on earth to justify a continuously anxious spirit.

Understandably, Paul is asking a lot here. There is nothing on earth that we will ever experience that should give us appropriate cause for prolonged anxiety. Why then, do we experience so much anxiety about what we go through?

As we will see in the next few days, this is our goal: to daily reflect on the goodness of God in light of our present situation. Remember, yesterday we were learning to rejoice always. If we spend our time rejoicing in the Lord in all situations, we are not constantly tempted to be anxious about what we see on the horizon.

I'm well aware that this feels impossible. The enormity of the statement to not be anxious in anything leaves me saying, "Paul, have you experienced what I'm going through right now?" But I'm also reminded of what Paul went through and was going through as he sat in his jail cell writing to the Philippian church. Paul had quite a few reasons to be anxious. He could very well be left and forgotten in prison. His life was constantly threatened, yet he writes to the Philippians—and to us—to not be anxious about anything.

We can readily understand the ramifications of this. If we are to rejoice always, we aren't to be anxious about anything.

We can overcome anxiety by reminding ourselves of He who has already overcome.

As believers, we have the full story, the full picture. The Bible gives us the story from beginning to end—from creation to victory. We can rest assured that while uneasiness reigns on earth, a day is coming when all will be made new and right. We can read from Genesis to Revelation and see the unfolding story of God's redemption on earth. This is the good news of the gospel message.

As difficult as it may be, we must train our minds to remember the temporal nature of our distress and that Christ has overcome the world (John 16:33). If we are in Christ, we are secure in the Victor.

Today, do not work to numb your mind to the anxiety you feel. If you are overwhelmed by the anxiety and situations you face, spend time focusing not on your stress, but rejoicing in your own salvation through Christ. Remind yourself of the temporary nature of your affliction and the eternal security you can rest in, through Christ.

Day 5

Prescriptive Prayer

"*Do not be anxious about anything,* but in everything by prayer and supplication *with thanksgiving let your requests be made known to God.*"

—Philippians 4:6, author's emphasis

•   •   •   •   •

. . . . .

If not being anxious about anything is our goal, Paul now gives the prescription for how we truly live anxiety-free.

Paul declares that if we are to not be anxious about anything, then we pray about *everything*. If we mix prayer with rejoicing and add thanksgiving, we have a recipe for living free from our anxious tendencies.

Again, like a well-crafted family recipe, it takes practice and discipline to truly perfect. Our most natural response is to curl up and sink into the pit of despair; however, we have the most basic formula for dealing with anxiety and living with the peace of God.

We pray.

We pray about everything.

It is good for us, at times, to step away from the routine we have established and pray. Jesus often retreated from His disciples, went to a quiet place, and prayed. Likewise, we should take these overwhelming matters, retreat from the normal, and lift up all of these anxieties off of our own shoulders. If we are not intentional about praying in all circumstances, we will get carried away on the heels of our anxieties instead of releasing them onto shoulders that can carry them all.

Yesterday, as we looked at the enormity of not being anxious about anything, we can also see the enormity in praying about everything. If Paul writes that we pray about everything, it should encourage our hearts that God actually desires to hear us pray about everything. He cares and desires for us to bring Him the minutia and struggles of our days to Him.

There's nothing in our world outside the realm of His sovereign care.

God allows us to make known our needs and requests. We pray and petition what is on our hearts, asking God to conform us into His image and align us with His divine will. Because we have been given this opportunity to lift up our prayers and petitions, we shouldn't be shy to ask God for the needs of our hearts.

But let me caution you not to predetermine your desired answer before you bring forth your supplication. God listens, hears, and responds to our requests. We must be careful to let Him, in His sovereign long-seeing will, answer our prayers. And if we are to submit our lives to Him in everything, we must accept His plan over our own, even if His response seems delayed or opposite of our fleeting desire.

If we believe God is good, then we must trust that His plan is good, even if it deviates from what we may think is best.

Day 6
Finding Thankfulness

"Do not be anxious about anything, but in everything by prayer and supplication with thanksgiving *let your requests be made known to God."*

—Philippians 4:6, author's emphasis

· · · · ·

· · · · ·

Our prayers should be bound together with threads of thankfulness. In all things, we are able and encouraged to give thanks.

Thankfulness is the conduit by which we can release ourselves of the burdens of worry, fear, and envy. Despite your current circumstance, you have a great deal to be thankful for. Though these blessings may not be directly in front of us or even near to our eyes, we must purposefully dwell in thankfulness.

In the first few years of our marriage, my wife and I lived in six different homes. I'm not even quite sure how it happened, but in each of those years, like clockwork, we packed up our things and moved—sometimes across town and sometimes across the state. We finally were able to move out of an apartment and rent a home. We were thrilled to be in a house for the first time as a married couple. It was a simple joy that we were so thankful for.

Six months into our time in that home, our house was broken into. Our hearts sunk as we walked through with the police, searching for any evidence and taking stock of what was missing. It was a sense of violation I had never felt before. We no longer looked at our home as a place of safety and security. What we were once so thankful for had shifted and became a source of anxiety.

Eventually, we were able to shift our focus and stayed in the house. Six months more passed, and we came home from work to find our house burglarized again. As we went through the motions with the officers again, we knew we couldn't stay any longer. Everything had changed.

What was once a tremendous source of thankfulness was now a source of anxiety and trepidation. It was nearly impossible to continue to give thanks that we had a home to go to—until someone reminded me of the simple facts of the situation.

We had a home to rest our heads in at night.

We had a home to keep us warm from the rain and elements.

We had a home to have friends over for community.

We had a home to invest in relationships with others.

We had a home to build memories.

And we would find another place to call home. This was not the end.

As always, circumstances will change, but we can find thankful moments tucked away in everything. All situations breed moments for thankfulness. Some more apparent than others, nonetheless, we must be diligent in finding woven into each of our days the ways in which we can thank God for His provision, guidance, direction, love, and mercy.

At the end of the day, those in Christ have salvation for which we can give thanks constantly. If you lack anything in regard to thankfulness, be encouraged that you have been eternally secure in a most loving God, who has redeemed and restored your soul.

Bind your prayers together with this thankfulness: that in Christ, God so loved you that He made you alive eternally.

Day 7

Lift Up Your Voice

"Do not be anxious about anything, but in everything by prayer and supplication with thanksgiving let your requests be made known to God."

—Philippians 4:6, author's emphasis

• • • • •

· · · · ·

In our greatest storms, it can be difficult to muster much of a voice. We need so much—and feel so overwhelmed and so lost—that coming to God to present our needs feels far too arduous a task.

The days that followed Mom's diagnosis were tumultuous. There were extreme ups and downs. There were times when I felt completely at peace and ready to take on the future but also times when the only response I could muster was to lie prostrate on the floor, full of tears, and voiceless. I couldn't pray. I couldn't think. I felt the immensity of the situation flood like a tidal wave over my soul.

Those moments taught me more about the God I serve and His nearness to those who are hurting. I knew in those moments of deepest strife and pain that God was near to my broken heart. I did not lay alone in my fear, but I had a God who was near, allowing His power to be made perfect while I was in my weakest state.

Let's remind ourselves together that we do not serve a God who sits enthroned and separated from His people.

For we do not have a high priest who is unable to sympathize with our weaknesses, but one who in every respect has been tempted as we are, yet without sin. Let us then with confidence draw near to the throne of grace, that we may receive mercy and find grace to help in time of need.
—Hebrews 4:15–16

Jesus, our faithful High Priest, beckons us to approach His throne with humble confidence, knowing that in Him we can find help in our times of greatest need.

This is a beautiful and humbling reminder for us. God is concerned with our strife. He hears and does not abandon us. Our requests are not too small for His ear. As He is over all things, small and large, your biggest and smallest needs are welcome before His throne.

When you imagine a king sitting on his throne, what sorts of things do you think about? Do you imagine the common citizen has access to him? Do you imagine the king welcoming servants and commoners to his throne? Do you think the king would want to know the everyday needs of each of the people under his lordship?

Think on the King we serve. Our Ruler welcomes His people to His throne because of what Christ has done. Our

Lord has asked His people to confidently approach His courts. And what can we expect to find there?

Empty promises?

Guilt?

Condemnation?

No.

We can expect to find mercy and grace in our time of need. This is the divine promise the writer of Hebrews expresses to us. God's throne is full of grace, not condemnation. We can present our needs—small and large—to our God, releasing them from our own power and into His divine goodness.

DAY 8

A GUARD IN CHRIST

"And the peace of God, which surpasses all understanding, will guard your hearts and your minds in Christ Jesus."

—Philippians 4:7

·　·　·　·　·

• • • • •

We find peace when we allow Christ—not ourselves—to guard our hearts and minds. When we relinquish control of our situations and rely on His strength over our own, we are filled with the transcending peace of God instead of temporary reprieve.

In the course of just a few short months, life seemed to crumble, and I realized how little control I had. Mom's cancer diagnosis was preceded by one of my nephews being rushed to the hospital with seizures. Along the same time, our home was broken into for the second time, forcing us to move into my aunt and uncle's basement. Weeks later, another family member had an accident, driving their car 20 feet into a home and somehow walking away without a scratch. Throughout all of this, my wife was also searching for a job, and we were searching for a new home.

We felt the full weight of being out of control. The only conceivable choice we could make was to stop, relax, and rely on God's plan in the midst of the turmoil. We could not control these events swirling around, but we could maintain a peace, trusting in God's provision over our uncertainty.

I still struggle with holding too tightly to the rein of my life, but I know that He will guard our hearts and minds in Christ Jesus. Whatever we've built will struggle to withstand the wind and rain if we've built it without a solid foundation.

This verse in Philippians 4:7 is often quoted in isolation from its context as encouragement when someone is dealing with difficulty, but the words Paul wrote before and after give this verse its incredible weight. This is the house that we hope to build, what comes before and after is the foundation that we lay it upon.

A strong foundation is the goal of our daily spiritual journey, that we may find a peace that surpasses the natural rationale of our difficult situations.

God's peace is limitless and bountiful.

The peace we create is bound by circumstance.

We desperately need the peace God provides to guard our hearts and minds. We know that as difficulty increases, our minds wander into places that make us even more fearful of the future. The ocean begins to rage tidal waves in our mind, sending ripples to every crevice in our brain. Our hearts hurt with countless thoughts stemming from what we see in our difficulty. We have surely experienced a measure of this in our lives and understand the importance of Christ guarding over our hearts and minds.

This is why it is critical that we take every thought captive and make it obedient to Christ (2 Corinthians 10:5). Our minds need peace in the goodness of God amidst our turbulence, not more distractions from His face. We take those thoughts, and we give them over to the divine purpose of God, not to the imperfect plans of our hearts and minds.

Relinquish control, rest in Him, and rely on His goodness in your life.

May the God of hope fill you with all joy and peace in believing, so that by the power of the Holy Spirit you may abound in hope.

—Romans 15:13

Day 9

Thinking Truth

"Finally, brothers, whatever is true, *whatever is honorable, whatever is just, whatever is pure, whatever is lovely, whatever is commendable, if there is any excellence, if there is anything worthy of praise, think about these things."*

—Philippians 4:8, author's emphasis

• • • • •

· · · · ·

Each circumstance we come to in life also ushers in an infinite number of possibilities for our minds to navigate. A major life decision brings to the surface feelings of inadequacy, regret for past mistakes, or fear of future failures.

We must guard ourselves by thinking on true things, versus lies or fears, in light of uncertainty.

When we had the opportunity to move to a new city for my wife, Brittany, to finish school, I had many months to prepare and find a job. At first, this brought excitement, as I knew God would lead us and direct me to that place where I could serve in the pastoral role to which I had been called. As time went on, no jobs opened and every door of opportunity seemed to slam shut. It left me reevaluating our decision to move and even questioning what God had called me to do. It was there I felt the tension of dwelling on the truth versus listening to lies about the good things God had called me to do in a new city. Ultimately, God was preparing the right place at the right time. We mustn't fear the future or buy into the lies about God: that He delays, forgets, or abandons. In the long arc of time, we will find the true meaning of what we are going through.

In Philippians 4:8, Paul gives a final encouragement on the state of our minds. He encourages us to think on things that are certain—over uncertain circumstances. His first desire is that we would focus on what is true.

Remember, the ruler of this world is the father of all lies. In the Garden of Eden, the primary focus of the deceiver was to spit subtle lies to undermine the authority and goodness of God. We are not naive to the schemes of our enemy. He will subtly and convincingly work his way into our minds, if we allow it.

Eve listened and pondered on the serpent's subtle deception. Adam, also knowing the truth, bit into the fruit of deception along with his wife. If we are not careful, in our vulnerable state we can see our circumstances and believe the lies of the enemy. We must be vigilant to watch and guard our minds from these attacks. When we are lowest, we are most vulnerable to deception. Lies about God's love, His care, His attentiveness to our needs, His proximity to us, His goodness, and His faithfulness will be the primary messages used to undermine our trust in the Lord.

We must think and dwell on truth, not on the subtle lies that distract us from the primary function of our struggles. God has *purpose* in our pain. He hasn't left or forsaken us. Do not bite into the fruit of deception that our God, the God of all peace and comfort, has left or denied our cries in our darkest hours.

The truth of Scripture is that we find God nearest to those that are hurting most.

When the righteous cry for help, the LORD hears and delivers them out of all their troubles. The LORD is near to the brokenhearted and saves the crushed in spirit.

—Psalm 34:17–18

Peace comes as we recognize and rest in the truth about God.

He is near to you.

Amidst your pain, trials, chaos, struggles, and frustration, He is near.

Take comfort in a God who is near and fasten your mind to the truth of Scripture.

Day 10

Peace in Justice

"Finally, brothers, whatever is true, whatever is honorable, whatever is just, whatever is pure, whatever is lovely, whatever is commendable, if there is any excellence, if there is anything worthy of praise, think about these things."

—Philippians 4:8, author's emphasis

· · · · ·

. . . . .

When we received the diagnosis about Mom's cancer, thoughts about the injustice of it all came flooding in my mind. In my eyes, my mother is a saint. She is the sweetest, most loving, and caring individual I've ever known. Yet, she had cancer. I thought, *Surely there are other people who would deserve to have cancer because of their nature.*

What a horrid thought! To see it in writing makes me feel worse that it crossed my mind often in those first few weeks. The diagnosis seemed in no way fair or just. God surely had the wrong person. Mom did not deserve this! We, as a family, didn't deserve to go through this pain. This was not the justice I believed we were due.

When Paul reminds us to dwell on what is honorable and just, he reminds us about the just God that we serve. It may be difficult to think thatwhat we face is just, but if we believe in the truth of Scripture, we can trust in a just and merciful God.

The wrath of God was poured out on Jesus because of our sin, giving us redemption of our sins past, present, and future. Because of our sin, the penalty we deserve is death, but God has provided His Son as payment for our sins. He has provided a way for us to be righteous in the sight of God.

Without the Cross, we stand hopeless before God. But, justice came on the Cross, to redeem a people cut off by sin.

This is the justice we didn't deserve but received. In these terms—remembering the Cross—illness, sickness, struggle, and pain are but a fleeting obstruction on the road to sanctification and grace.

He has shown his people the power of his works,
in giving them the inheritance of the nations.
The works of his hands are faithful and just; all
his precepts are trustworthy; they are established
forever and ever, to be performed with faithful-
ness and uprightness. He sent redemption to his
people; he has commanded his covenant forever.
Holy and awesome is his name!

—Psalm 111:6–9

I know the depth of difficulty in understanding why God chooses to allow certain things to occur in the world. Many times it does not make sense, and we are left frustrated and angry at God for what He has allowed. It certainly does not feel fair or just to us. I cannot begin to answer the questions all of us have in our spirits about the nature and plan of God, but what we may never know on this side of heaven may be apparent to us in eternity. His plan is not to harm but to prosper (Jeremiah 29:11). His plan is working all things together for the good of those who love Him and are called according to His purpose (Romans 8:28). While we may not see that perfect purpose now, in a month, in a year, or even in this lifetime, as we remain faithful, we will see our God completing a good work in us.

And we know that for those who love God all things work together for good, for those who are called according to his purpose.

—Romans 8:28

Day 11

Unnumb

*"Finally, brothers, whatever is true,
whatever is honorable, whatever is just,*
whatever is pure, whatever is lovely,
whatever is commendable, *if there is any
excellence, if there is anything worthy of
praise, think about these things."*

— Philippians 4:8, author's emphasis

. . . . .

• • • • •

You cannot turn on a television or browse the Internet without being reminded of the overwhelming amount of trash the world consumes. Everywhere we turn, we are pounded with impurity after impurity. Worse yet, it can hit us without warning from any direction. It is nearly inescapable.

Where do we turn to find pure, lovely, and commendable things to think on?

One of the most important things we can do to dwell in purity is to fight to guard our minds from the mess of the world. Strife breeds opportunity for our minds to be indulged in numbing agents. We desperately want to be numb to difficulty happening to us, but there is hope for something better than just being numb. We can be full of joy and peace in the world while we walk this path of strife.

The words of the LORD are pure words, like silver refined in a furnace on the ground, purified seven times.

—Psalm 12:6

Dwelling in God's pure, Holy Word is the perfect place to rest in truth and find confidence to stand. Instead of flipping on the television, getting lost in a book, or mindlessly browsing the Internet, focus your heart, mind, and soul on the purity of God's Word. It won't be a numbing experience, but may awaken your soul.

In my life, I wrestle constantly, trying desperately to avoid the uncomfortable scenarios playing out in my mind. I would far rather turn on the television or browse the Internet than face the difficulty. Technology, food, drink, and media all provide the escape many of us crave. Escape is accessible anytime, from any place, during any circumstance. If we are not careful, we exchange the peace of God for a numbness of mind.

It is much easier to be numb than to face our problems and intentionally submit them to our heavenly Father. And it is far easier to enjoy what the world can temporarily offer than to take joy in the Lord of life and the Giver of all peace.

The easier path is to turn off and be filled by the scraps of the world, but the Word of God will not leave us hungry. It is living water, pure, and full of promises by which we can stand in the face of our trials (John 4:14). We can stand not on our own might and power, but in the purity of the promise of God's holy nature.

Day 12

Peaceful Sustenance

"Finally, brothers, whatever is true, whatever is honorable, whatever is just, whatever is pure, whatever is lovely, whatever is commendable, if there is any excellence, if there is anything worthy of praise, think about these things."

—Philippians 4:8, author's emphasis

· · · · ·

• • • • •

I recently came down with a horrible stomach bug. It was a miserable few days and nights of relentless discomfort. Once the stomachaches subsided and I had shed the virus, it was time to slowly begin to eat real foods again. The best way to get my strength back was to start with pure, natural foods. It would have been unthinkable for me, after being sick in bed for days, to attempt to regain strength by eating a greasy hamburger, drinking soda, and munching on candy. Regaining my health started with feeding my body staples such as water, bread, and rice. Our bodies' health often comes from what we feed on. Our minds' health also comes from what we feed on.

Paul tells his readers to think about those things that sustain and nourish you—things that are worthy of your thoughts. Don't allow your mind to wander to places that leave you morose, troubled, and weak.

Our thoughts often drive our actions. More importantly, feeding our minds nourishing thoughts is essential in preparing us for whatever comes our way, whether we are in a season of blessings or a season of great discomfort. In every circumstance, we must be diligent to digest those pure, lovely, and commendable things that we find in Scripture and through prayer.

If we "zoom out" and look at what Paul is asking, we may feel overwhelmed by what Paul is asking. Pray about everything. Don't be anxious about anything. Only think about pure and godly things. But Paul is not speaking on principles he is unfamiliar with. He is giving us the secret that he has personally found to be true.

Paul experienced a great measure of distress in his own life. Along with every other apostle that followed Jesus in the New Testament story, comfort and peaceful living was not part of his job description. There was no relaxing by the beach to find peace. There was certainly no retreating to quiet vacation homes for months on end to relieve the stress of sharing Christ with the world.

But Paul and the rest of the apostles maintained peace despite imprisonment, illness, threats, and injustice happening directly to them.

When we read Paul's words, we know we are reading words from a man who has learned what having a peace that surpasses understanding truly means. We aren't hearing it from secondhand sources, researchers, or theorists.

An unmanufactured, God-given peace comes when we strive for Philippians 4:7 by living Philippians 4:5–8. These verses bundled together give us a foundation by which we can find the peace of God.

It's not easy to stop our anxiety and focus on our prayers.

It's not natural to be thankful in moments of crisis.

It's not intuitive to fix our eyes on Jesus when the storms are brewing.

But this is Paul's steadfast call to find an unnatural peace in a God who willingly gives.

Day 13

Simply Rest

*"In peace I will both lie down and sleep;
for you alone, O LORD, make me dwell
in safety."*

—Psalm 4:8

The first night after our house got broken into, I lay awake nearly the entire night, my adrenaline pumping, listening for any abnormality in the house. Our security had been breached only a few hours before, and I did not have much trust that it would not be breached again. I put our refrigerator in front of the door that had been kicked in, hoping to prevent the entry of any would-be intruder, and we kept most of the lights on in the living room.

Sleep was so elusive during those first few nights as I lay awake, fearful of what might happen. But sleep is usually elusive when there is fear and trepidation about something that might be forthcoming. We hope for peaceful sleep, but often nighttime brings only restlessness and mindless wanderings, filled with fear and anxiety.

Psalm 4:8 describes something altogether different. King David is able to lie down and sleep, in peace, with knowledge of his enemies and critics lurking nearby with his destruction in mind. Despite knowing that there was unrest and potential danger present, David confidently slept.

I see a king who understood his orientation. He may have sat on a powerful throne and been the king of Israel, but he was confident not in his own power but in the power of God. David knew he could not fabricate enough security or safety to keep his mind at ease, but he could place his trust in the Lord and allow Him to provide peace over fear.

"For you alone, O Lord." Nothing else can give us this peace. David could have easily called in guards and placed them outside his doors. He could have numbed his mind with drink and wine. He could have done countless things to take his mind off the present circumstance, but David chose to place his trust in the only One able to give him peace in the midst of joy and stress.

Likewise, we can turn our attention to innumerable distractions or safety precautions, but only God gives us perfect peace.

Knowing the goodness of the Lord and His steadfast love, we can receive the peace of God in any and every circumstance. We can find rest for our weary souls and our tired bodies as we place our confidence in the One who keeps us safe and gives peace to His people.

Day 14

Shepherding Peace

*"The LORD is my shepherd; I shall not want.
He makes me lie down in green pastures. He
leads me beside still waters. He restores my
soul. He leads me in paths of righteousness
for his name's sake. Even though I walk
through the valley of the shadow of death,
I will fear no evil, for you are with me;
your rod and your staff, they comfort me."*

—Psalm 23:1–4

• • • • •

• • • • •

This past Christmas, the adults in the small church I pastor put on a short play for the kids. It was neat to watch the children see their moms and dads play the parts of angels, shepherds, and wise men. The children's little eyes glowed in fascination as they hung on to the words of the story as it played out in front of them.

As I narrated the story, I noticed something that I had neglected to notice before in Scripture. It may have been the set that we had made or *The Jesus Storybook Bible* I was reading aloud for the first time, but there was something striking in the juxtaposition of the heralding angels alongside the longtime shepherds.

It is one of the most fascinating tidbits from the familiar Christmas story—that the shepherds were the first people to hear the good news that Jesus was born. Countless thousands of angels appeared to the shepherds, heralding the good news of what was coming.

The image of glorious angels of light singing to dirty, smelly shepherds in the dark is one of the most beautiful images of the coming gospel.

The first people to greet the newborn Savior were unclean shepherd outcasts. Jesus was born, turned away from the inn, and greeted by outcast shepherds. He then spent His short life on earth loving outcasts and finally died the death of a criminal to redeem those cast out by sin.

But there's more to the story. God shows us something else in the shepherds' story. Not only did Jesus spend His life ministering to the downtrodden and those people who were rejected by society, but He would also become our great Shepherd, leading, guiding, and protecting us. Bringing us, the outcasts due to sin, into the loving arms of our God.

He himself bore our sins in his body on the tree,

that we might die to sin and live to righteousness.

By his wounds you have been healed. For you

were straying like sheep, but have now returned

to the Shepherd and Overseer of your souls.

—1 Peter 2:24–25

The Lord became our Shepherd, guiding us through life's great trials. He is with us, comforting us with His provision and protection.

Even as we walk through the greatest of life's fears, we can walk confidently with our Shepherd, knowing that He is able to guide us through.

We have no reason to fear but, rather, every reason to carry on. We know our Shepherd is with us. His rod and staff, the Shepherd's greatest tools to ward off attacks on His sheep, are ready to overcome whatever comes our way.

Just like a shepherd carefully watches and guides his sheep to safe pasture, our Lord will lead and guide us through rocky and dry stretches to lead us to safe and green pastures.

DAY 15

A REIGN OF PEACE

"The LORD sits enthroned over the flood;
the LORD sits enthroned as king forever.
May the LORD give strength to his people!
May the LORD bless his people with peace!"

—Psalm 29:10–11

• • • • •

· · · · ·

When we experience uncertain circumstances, it can be difficult to see the Lord's hand at work. As Mom was diagnosed with cancer and began her treatments, it was challenging trying to find God's divine hand at work. But Scripture speaks about God's enthronement over all things, big and small. His divine plan works in ways that are far superior to our plans (Isaiah 55:8–9).

From the rains of a flood to the cancer forming from a single mutated cell, nothing falls outside the reign of our God.

I see the inherent difficulty of this truth. Mom's cancer is not outside the Lord's control. The flood that wiped out the earth in the time of Noah was certainly not outside God's control. The events He has allowed to occur do not define His proximity to us and our circumstances. Yes, God allowed pancreatic cancer in Mom's body, but that does not mean He has left us without hope. We'll never understand the cancer diagnosis, but we have been eternally grateful for the peace, strength, and hope that He has graciously given.

We prayed hard for healing, thinking that was our greatest need for Mom. That was our greatest want, but our greatest need was really peace and strength to hear news and make decisions going forward. God granted peace and a strength that prevailed in the face of despairing news. God's nearness to our family during that time in our life produced an intimacy with the Father that I, personally, had not experienced before. True, I did not fully understand His plan, but I knew He was near.

Mom's healing did not come instantaneously, but God blessed her with what she needed to undergo the difficult journey of chemotherapy. While we steadily prayed for our greatest desire, which was healing, He was delivering to her and to us our greatest need—peace that surpassed our belief. He blessed her with peace that enabled her to walk forward into the unknown, day after day.

I am so thankful for a God who graciously provides for our greatest needs. We have a God who sits over everything, knowing all, seeing all, and loving us the same.

The psalmist describes beautifully the Lord sitting enthroned. We can remind ourselves that He reigns over the floods, droughts, joys, sorrows, cancer, and health, and He will provide strength and bless His people with peace to endure whatever comes our way.

Day 16

A Strong Tower

*"The name of the LORD is a strong tower;
the righteous man runs into it and is safe."*

—Proverbs 18:10

. . . . .

• • • • •

We have a lot of tornadoes where I live and work in central Alabama. Many of the tornadoes have left extensive damage to the landscape of many cities in our area. When the tornado warnings are relayed through TV, radio, and social media, everybody knows exactly where to go to find their safe place.

At home, we scurry to our basements and inner sanctuaries. At work, we go to our designated locations deep within the building. When the tornadoes come, we go to the strongest place we can find.

In much the same way, when the storms of life come our way, where will we run to find safety? Where is the strongest shelter from the storm?

Why would we choose to seek shelter in a house made of straw or find covering from rain under a tree? These are not strong, and they are not safe. We know the name of the Lord is a strong tower, providing safety for those who run into it. Knowing this is where we find safety, why should we continue to run to those things that do not provide safety and allow for peace?

Often, the safest and most peaceful places may be in our prayer closets in the presence of the Lord. We can trust in the name of the Lord not to fail us when we need Him most. We can trust in Him to provide us peace no matter the power of the storm we face. We only run to Him and take refuge in Him. Psalm 91 continues this thought when the psalmist writes:

He who dwells in the shelter of the Most High
will abide in the shadow of the Almighty. I will
say to the LORD, "My refuge and my fortress, my
God, in whom I trust." For he will deliver you
from the snare of the fowler and from the deadly
pestilence. He will cover you with his pinions,
and under his wings you will find refuge; his
faithfulness is a shield and buckler.
—Psalm 91:1–4

Be encouraged today. When danger begins to loom, run to the Lord to find safety. He has not left us to fend for ourselves but has provided a place of refuge and strength for us to run into. There is a prevalent peace in the safety of our God.

Day 17

Lift Up Your Eyes

"I lift up my eyes to the hills. From where does my help come? My help comes from the LORD, who made heaven and earth."

—Psalm 121:1–2

· · · · ·

．．．．．

Do you remember that feeling when you got busted—caught in the act of misbehavior as a young child? There were more than a few times that have been forever engrained in my memory when I got caught in a lie or blatantly disobeyed my parents. It was rough, and there was never anywhere sufficient to hide.

Little children have a tough time hiding their emotions. As the old saying goes, they wear their emotions on their sleeves. If they are upset, they'll let you know. If they are sad, their heads hang low and their eyes chase the ground. I must admit, I'm guilty of the same thing as an adult. When life becomes unbearably burdensome and I feel defeated, my instinct is to lower my head and become downcast.

It's an instinctual humility that comes out when our heads tuck and our eyes dip. We admit that we have lost or been overtaken by something.

But . . . the psalmist says he lifts his eyes up to the hills and asks the rhetorical question, "Where does my help come from?" It is quite easy to be downcast, head down, eyes to the ground, saddened by all the circumstances around.

If our eyes are fixated on the earth, we quickly lose focus on our heavenly help.

As soon as our eyes hit the ground, we must quickly remind ourselves where our help comes from. Our help is not found on the earth. It isn't found in things, objects, or people. Our help only comes from the Lord.

Turn your gaze upward, knowing that there is hope ahead. Your help and my help is upward and founded in the Lord, Maker of heaven and earth. The sovereign Lord, Creator of all things we see, is our help in times of strife.

Don't hang your head in defeat. Lift your eyes to the hills, knowing that you have help. You are not alone and you are not relegated to the depth of the valley.

Read Psalm 121 in its entirety:

I lift up my eyes to the hills. From where does my help come? My help comes from the LORD, who made heaven and earth. He will not let your foot be moved; he who keeps you will not slumber. Behold, he who keeps Israel will neither slumber nor sleep. The LORD is your keeper; the LORD is your shade on your right hand. The sun shall not strike you by day, nor the moon by night. The Lord will keep you from all evil; he will keep your life. The LORD will keep your going out and your coming in from this time forth and forevermore.

Remind yourself of the truth of Psalm 121. Lift your gaze upward, and put your trust and hope in the Lord. He will strengthen, comfort, and keep you.

Day 18

Relief

"Answer me when I call, O God of my righteousness! You have given me relief when I was in distress. Be gracious to me and hear my prayer!"

—Psalm 4:1

. . . . .

• • • • •

I may not look the part currently, but there was a day when I lifted weights multiple times a week. I never enjoyed the task, but I knew it was necessary in training for sports. One of the activities I did each week was the bench press. I would lift the weights while my teammate would spot and help, in case my strength failed to lift the heavy bar and weights over my chest. This spotter was a great help so many times as I would increase the weight on the sides of the bar. There was a wonderful feeling of relief the moment the spotter placed his hands on the bar and helped lift the bar alongside me.

As a culture, we love the idea and feeling of relief. Commercials barrage us with messages wooing us to find relief from pain, hunger, extra pounds, and stress. From the time of the psalmists to the present day, we are constantly seeking relief from the pains of the world. Debt-relief companies are booming, disaster-relief organizations are engaged all over the world, and other agencies aid individuals through their various struggles.

Couldn't we all just use a little relief?

King David's story is one that has great peaks and tremendous valleys. He goes through great trials and great triumphs. Yet, he understood where his relief came from. As the king of a land with immense resources, David could easily have numbed his distress with drink, entertainment, music, or people; however, he cried out to the God of his righteousness for relief.

When distress came David's way, he did not look to what the world could provide; he looked to what only his God could provide.

So the question becomes: Where do we turn when we are in distress? As we have read before, our tendency is to seek worldly and temporal treasures to numb our pain and relax our mind's constant churning. These agents work temporarily as they dull our senses to reality. In the meantime, we miss the call of our God who David beckons in prayer in Psalm 4. The Lord will provide relief for us.

We forgo the reality of peace for fleeting pleasures that only mask the underlying need.

When life comes crashing down, where do you turn? When difficult times come your way, do you run to the world or do you cling to your Father?

. . . .

God is our refuge and strength, a very present help in trouble. Therefore we will not fear though the earth gives way, though the mountains be moved into the heart of the sea, though its waters roar and foam, though the mountains tremble at its swelling.

—Psalm 46:1–3

. . . .

DAY 19
FIND REST

"Come to me, all who labor and are heavy laden, and I will give you rest."

—Matthew 11:28

. . . . .

• • • • •

If we are honest with ourselves and look deep into our spirit, we have countless burdens weighing heavily upon us. Questions swirling in our minds: *How will I pay this bill? Where will my kids go to school? How will we afford that? What if we get sick? Can I do this?* The list goes on and on and on. It is exhausting when we pause long enough to sit, think, and process all the questions and burdens on our shoulders. Burdens of work, home, school, children, marriage, family—all well up with unknowns and uncertainties.

But in all of that is one unshakeable certainty—our God.

Even as I write this paragraph, I have multiple areas in life that are overwhelming my mind. I am exhausted trying to hold up each of these concerns, giving them immense weight in my heart. My mind is weary. My heart is weary. And my soul is weary as I have taken the weight of my worries solely on my own shoulders.

In the midst of all these worries, fears, and unknowns, our Lord simply says, "Come to me and you will find rest." We can dwell in the land of our burdens, or we can run into the arms of the Lord to find peace and rest.

At points in life, rest is one of the hardest things to attain. We hustle and bustle from one chore to the next, one appointment to another. We worry about one thing after the next. Some Bible translations exchange "labor and heavy laden" for "weary and burdened" (NIV) in Matthew 11:28. Jesus calls those who are weary with the world to come to Him to find rest.

We need rest when we carry too many of our own burdens.

This verse is not necessarily referring to physical exhaustion. Rather, it speaks to the times we feel the weight of our pain, struggles, and difficulties, when we become weary and heavy laden—and peace is a distant dream. At these times, Jesus, the Creator and Sustainer of all things, beckons us to come to Him to find rest. There, in the embrace of our God, we find perfect peace and perfect rest for our overburdened souls.

Understand that carrying the weight of your own worries is unsustainable. Not only is it unsustainable, it is not spiritually healthy. We have a gracious God who calls us to come to Him in our tired and weary state to find the rest that we so desperately need.

DAY 20

RELEASE CONTROL

"'God opposes the proud but gives grace to the humble.' Humble yourselves, therefore, under the mighty hand of God so that at the proper time he may exalt you."

—1 Peter 5:5–6

· · · · ·

· · · · ·

For the next few days, we will look at 1 Peter 5:5–11, one of the most helpful passages of Scripture as we struggle through life's difficulties. At the onset of this passage, we see the proper orientation God directs for our lives. God opposes the proud, but He gives grace to those who are humble.

I am in a constant battle with my own pride. My sin flows from the pride that wells within me. At times, this sin manifests itself into the false belief that I am more capable of handling my problems than God is. I have found myself searching for my own solace instead of enjoying the perfect peace of God. I have mistakenly tried to fix those problems that only God can remedy. And I have wearily attempted to figure out the details of my future rather than rest in God's faithful provision. Pride always blocks a right relationship with God. It hinders a fully submitted rest and reliance on God to provide what only He can.

We find grace and peace in God when we fully realize that we are incapable of finding these things outside of our relationship with our Creator.

When we are humbled before God, we understand that we need God to reign in our lives. We accept He is in control. We rejoice that He has a divine plan for our lives. We trust that He is good. We put our faith in believing that He is working all things together for good (Romans 8:28). And we also fully recognize we are under His sovereign care.

To be in opposition to God is a frightening thought. But that is precisely what occurs when we declare our own will, desires, needs, and expectations above the Creator and deny His care for us.

Why should God allow us a steadfast peace when we choose to be the sole rulers of our lives?

The process of humbling ourselves before God is not something that is enjoyable or something that comes naturally. It is so very difficult to release control and trust God in our circumstances, but it is incredibly necessary that we work to surrender control and humble ourselves under the mighty hand of God.

Remember that the same mighty hand of God that created and sustained all things also welcomes us to Him, knowing that we can find rest for our weary souls.

This knowledge is the continual, daily foundation that we rest on. The foundation of faith in God, not ourselves, to see us through whatever we face. Begin today, laying down your life at the foot of the throne of a God who loves, cares, and carries us through the difficulties we face.

30 DAYS OF HOPE FOR PEACEFUL LIVING

Day 21

A God Who Cares

"Casting all your anxieties on him, because he cares for you."

—1 Peter 5:7

. . . . .

. . . . .

As we go through the process of humbling ourselves before God, we also see more hope in the nature of God. We see in Matthew 11:28 that if we are weary and burdened, we can find rest. Here in 1 Peter 5:7 we are also welcomed to cast all of our anxiety on God. Notice closely the word *all*. I am still struggling and holding onto those issues I anxiously want to control while releasing others into heaven. I need the constant reminder that we are able to cast all of our anxiety on God.

Not some.

Not just the small things.

Not only the big things.

But everything.

We can come to God with all of our anxiety. Anxieties from the day. Anxieties from failures. Anxieties from any facet of life are welcomed at the throne of God. This has to be great news to our ears. Our God is near enough to allow us to place our anxieties squarely on Him—not that He will take the circumstance away, but so we can place our trust in Him, knowing He is working these things together for good (Romans 8:28).

Why are we allowed this privilege with the Most High?

Because He cares for us. He cares for you.

Take a step back for just a moment. God, Creator of heaven and earth, cares for you.

But God, being rich in mercy, because of the great love with which he loved us, even when we were dead in our trespasses, made us alive together with Christ—by grace you have been saved—and raised us up with him and seated us with him in the heavenly places in Christ Jesus, so that in the coming ages he might show the immeasurable riches of his grace in kindness toward us in Christ Jesus.

—Ephesians 2:4–7

Due to the relationship we are able to have with God because of what Christ did on the Cross, we are capable of having incredible intimacy with the sovereign Lord.

Ephesians 2:4–7, paired with 1 Peter 5:7, shows us the reason behind why we can cast our anxieties on God and why He cares for us. We serve a God who loves His people and cares for them. We have access and intimacy with the sovereign God because of the reconciliatory effort of Christ on the Cross. The entire Bible speaks this good news to us.

30 DAYS OF HOPE for Peaceful Living

DAY 22
TWO CHOICES

"Be sober-minded; be watchful. Your adversary the devil prowls around like a roaring lion, seeking someone to devour."

—1 Peter 5:8

. . . . .

DAY 23
NOT ALONE

"Resist him, firm in your faith, knowing that the same kinds of suffering are being experienced by your brotherhood throughout the world."

—1 Peter 5:9

· · · · ·

. . . . .

One of the worst mistakes I made early in my marriage was agreeing to run a half marathon with my wife, Brittany. I prided myself on being a decently in-shape individual. I enjoy team sports, but I despise running without any seeming purpose. However, I wanted to be a good husband and do something together with her.

To gauge my own fitness level, I went out for a run one afternoon while Brittany was at work. I ran and ran for what felt like an eternity. As I hobbled back up to our front porch, I looked down at my smartphone's pedometer to see that I had run a little over one mile. I hobbled inside to recheck the distance of the half marathon. Thirteen miles. I had a problem.

The next few times we trained, Brittany and I ran together, and I was shocked at how much further I was able to run when she was next to me, enduring the pains together with me. I was even more shocked that I was able to finish the half marathon with her. I had a connection with her that pushed me to take the next step, knowing she and thousands of others were next to, behind, and in front of me. It gave me a drive to keep going.

Likewise, we can know that we are not suffering alone here on earth. The struggles we are dealing with are also being experienced by our brotherhood throughout the world. We can endure and take steps forward together, knowing we are not isolated in our struggles, but are united together in Christ.

If you are isolated in your circumstances, open yourself up to others to run the race along with you. We are not meant to journey through this life alone. We need people to remind us to put the first foot in front of the other and move forward. We need others to be in the trenches with us, fighting alongside us. Isolation will only lead us further into isolation.

Believers who came before you have felt the same pains you are feeling and have endured with Christ. Currently, believers are experiencing similar situations as you, and they are enduring in Christ. Be encouraged that you are not alone. Take heart in the community of believers around the world, who are enduring suffering for the sake of Christ.

Your endurance for the cause of Christ will be greater and stronger with others alongside you. Your willingness to take steps forward in faith will be more confident with like-minded souls encouraging you.

You are not alone. Our great Savior is with you, beckoning you to join the community of believers who will fight, struggle, and encourage you on in faith.

Therefore, since we are surrounded by so great a cloud of witnesses, let us also lay aside every weight, and sin which clings so closely, and let us run with endurance the race that is set before us, looking to Jesus, the founder and perfecter of our faith, who for the joy that was set before him endured the cross, despising the shame, and is seated at the right hand of the throne of God.
—Hebrews 12:1–2

DAY 24
RESPONDING TO SUFFERING

"And after you have suffered a little while."

—1 Peter 5:10

. . . . .

· · · · ·

I n a 30-day devotional about peace, this will not be one of the more enjoyable devotions to read, but the truth about suffering is clearly demonstrated throughout Scripture.

There were times, as I lay awake at night, that I wrestled with the why of this difficulty our family was facing. While what we went through pales in comparison to much of the suffering fellow believers around the world face, I struggled to fit my circumstances into my limited understanding of God's plan. I could not have guessed this pain would so clearly bring about a better understanding of God's peace.

As believers, we should not be surprised when suffering comes. While we may not embrace it with open arms, we can be prepared to respond in godly peace when it does arrive.

Peter says, "After you have suffered a little while." There is no mention of *if* but a clear indication that suffering *is* a normal and expected process in the Christian life. It is apparent to anyone who has lived for any amount of time that immunity to strife does not exist in this life. In a quick glance over the men and women of the Bible, one cannot escape the vast amounts of suffering experienced by godly pillars of the Christian faith.

The measure of our faith is not an indicator of our level of suffering. We are not immune to difficulty, struggle, temptation, and hardship due to how much faith we have. Nor are we granted more difficulty, struggle, temptation, and hardship based on how little faith we have. It is our faith that measures how those difficulties affect us.

In John 16:33, Jesus shares this truth with His disciples: "I have said these things to you, that in me you may have peace. In the world you will have tribulation. But take heart; I have overcome the world." This is a clear indication that tribulation will occur, but Jesus offers hope for peace through tribulation. In both passages, we can see that our pain is not outside the plan and purpose of God. We have hope to endure through Christ who has overcome the world and has provided peace in Himself.

Following Jesus does not entail a cloak of immunity against job loss, sickness, suffering, pain, sorrow, or grief. What we find is not an end to our problems but a hope to carry us through them.

It isn't pleasant, but it is a truth we need to grasp. We should not be surprised when suffering comes. Our response will steer the ship of our situation to rejoicing and peace or despair, isolation, and strife. Suffering never becomes easy to handle, but we can embrace the pain as transformative and temporal.

Peter declares the temporary nature when he says, "After we have suffered a little while." This little while may be days and weeks, or it could be months and years. But, remember, our suffering is merely temporary. It is "a little while" as we consider the eternal nature of our salvation.

DAY 25
GOD'S RESTORATION

"And after you have suffered a little while, the God of all grace, who has called you to his eternal glory in Christ, will himself restore, confirm, strengthen, and establish you. To him be the dominion forever and ever. Amen."

—1 Peter 5:10–11

· · · · ·

• • • • •

I've always heard the phrase, "light at the end of the tunnel." In school, people would remind me about the light at the end of the long journey through college and seminary. When we go through a long and difficult process, it is good to remind ourselves about the light that's at the end of the struggle. Doing so gives us hope and an assurance that what we are enduring is worth the pain.

We have a magnificent Light we can look to through our present trials. The God of all grace will Himself make us strong again. We may be weak now, but we can look forward to the strengthening the Lord will provide.

He will restore us.

He will confirm us.

He will strengthen us.

He will establish us.

After we have suffered a little while.

Pause for a moment and recognize who is the Giver of all these promises. In chaos, we are unable to restore ourselves. When we face difficulties, we are unable to adequately strengthen ourselves. When we undergo trials, we are unable to establish ourselves on a firm foundation. We rely not on ourselves but on the God of all grace. We rely and depend on God to give grace, peace, and mercy in our time of need.

Paul knows this all too well as he asks God for the thorn to be removed from his flesh. He writes:

But he said to me, "My grace is sufficient for
you, for my power is made perfect in weakness."
Therefore I will boast all the more gladly of my
weaknesses, so that the power of Christ may
rest upon me. For the sake of Christ, then,
I am content with weaknesses, insults, hardships,
persecutions, and calamities. For when I am
weak, then I am strong.

—2 Corinthians 12:9–10

Whatever we face, we can boldly boast in the power of God working in our lives. Not in what we are able to do but what God has done to give us peace, rest, strength, and a foundation. This is the promise God has given to us: He Himself will give us this foundation and strength.

Peter finishes this section with a doxology to a God who is perfectly in control. Some translations may say *dominion*, *power*, or *glory*. Peter assures us again of where our help comes from. It comes from a God who sits clearly in control. Sovereign over our circumstances and solely reigning over all things. Peter expresses the dominion of God from the past to the present and into the future.

In the same way, we can rest in the goodness of God, who provides for His people in the past, present, and future.

Find peace in His perfect reign over all and in His promise to restore, confirm, strengthen, and establish you.

Day 26

Peaceful Resolve

"Peace I leave with you; my peace I give to you. Not as the world gives do I give to you. Let not your hearts be troubled, neither let them be afraid."

—John 14:27

"I have said these things to you, that in me you may have peace. In the world you will have tribulation. But take heart; I have overcome the world."

—John 16:33

• • • • •

As Mom began her chemotherapy regimen for pancreatic cancer, we were incredibly uncertain how she would respond to the treatments. We were told she could expect to live three to six months without treatment and as long as a year with treatment. The cancer had spread to numerous other organs, so there was little hope the treatments would effectively eradicate everything, but we hoped it would slow the spread of the cancer enough to prolong her life.

I watched as God's peace reigned in her heart and mind during the treatments. She completely trusted in the sovereign plan of her heavenly Father, despite the pain and discomfort her body felt.

She later wrote these words for a blog (colorboxphotog raphers.com/praising-god-for-healing-update-on-jennys-cancer-journey) that featured my parents and their journey with cancer:

"I'll be the first to admit that there is no way to understand the providence of God! I know I have to trust Him by faith through the dark times as well as the good, never understanding the why of things, but trusting anyway. My simple mind can't figure it out, but I have to trust that He knows what is best, that He has a plan, and that His will will be done."

Jesus shared the words from John 16:33 shortly before His arrest and death on the Cross. I find it fascinating that as He stared a horrific death dead in the eyes, He was encouraging His disciples not to lose heart and to be resolute in the face of tribulation. How is it possible that our Lord was able to be at peace, knowing what would soon be coming?

I believe He completely trusted in the sovereign plan of His Father.

The peace Jesus had did not take away the suffering and pain of the Cross, but it allowed Him to confidently move forward into what would ultimately become our salvation. The peace that Christ gives to us allows us to look squarely in the face of the known or unknown realities of our lives and take confident steps forward, carried in the love and grace of God.

I am thankful that Mom demonstrated to us what it looks like to have perfect peace in a God who overcame sin, suffering, and death to secure our salvation. As she faced a difficult road, she was able to take comfort in the plan of God. This was her peace and it brought us even more peace as we walked alongside her.

Day 27
Storms

"And a great windstorm arose, and the waves were breaking into the boat, so that the boat was already filling. But he was in the stern, asleep on the cushion. And they woke him and said to him, 'Teacher, do you not care that we are perishing?' And he awoke and rebuked the wind and said to the sea, 'Peace! Be still!' And the wind ceased, and there was a great calm."

—Mark 4:37–41

• • • • •

The seas were raging, and Jesus was sleeping.

I can imagine the disciples' frustration as they frantically raced to keep the boat afloat from the oncoming water, and I can imagine them scurrying around, hoping Jesus would wake up and do something to save them. Can you hear their tone as they ask in bewilderment, "Do you not care that we are perishing?"

I am guilty of thoughts similar to the disciples'. I ask, "God do you not care that I'm struggling?" and wonder why He seems so distant. I am so focused on my strife that I miss His nearness and inclined ear.

This story is reminiscent of another found in Luke 10:38–42. Martha is working diligently in the house as her sister, Mary, sits quietly at the feet of Jesus, listening to His teaching. As Martha's frustration reaches its tipping point, she asks Jesus, "Do you not care that my sister has left me to serve alone?" (v. 40). Both Martha and the disciples completely missed Jesus in their midst and instead focused their gazes to the chores and raging seas.

When Jesus awoke in the boat, He simply spoke a few words, commanding the seas to be at peace. Mark then reports that "there was a great calm." I imagine everything immediately was simply calm—the wind, the waves, the boat, and more importantly the disciples. Everything and everyone was instantly calmed by the command of the Lord, who by the same verbal pronouncements brought forth all of creation.

The juxtaposition of the disciples and the seas is staggering. The presence of Jesus in the boat should have provided the peace the disciples needed, but the wind in their faces blinded their eyes from the Savior in their midst. Jesus surely wanted them to have faith, regardless of whether the storms gathered around the boat or the winds were calm and quiet.

The disciples' peace relied on the circumstances they perceived. They perceived chaos and therefore responded in chaos.

Jesus did not rely on any circumstance for His peace but instead relied on the power of God. Jesus was not worried or afraid of the crashing waves—He spoke and calmed the storms. He spoke the words I believe He desired for the disciples, "Peace! Be still!" This command, while directed at the seas, ceased the fear from the disciples.

Likewise, Jesus asks us, "Why are you so afraid?" If we trust in the perfect plan of God, why do we still fear? Why do we have so little peace when the Prince of Peace rests in our boats?

We've seen that the storms will come. Suffering and strife will be present in our lives, but we can have relief from our fear and be blessed with a perfect peace as we fully trust God's provision for us.

For God gave us a spirit not of fear but of power and love and self-control.

—2 Timothy 1:7

Day 28

Silent Fight

"The LORD will fight for you, and you have only to be silent."

—Exodus 14:14

· · · · ·

· · · · ·

Each week, as I walk up to the pulpit at my church, I am reminded of my need for the Lord to work through me. I am the opposite of everything I thought a good pastor should be: I am quiet, shy, and introverted. Yet, my calling is to preach in front of crowds, develop relationships with people I do not know, and disciple individuals. After a typical Sunday morning, I'm exhausted and drained. There is always that moment just before I walk up to begin my sermon where I think, *what in the world am I doing?*

But each week, God's power is made perfect in my weakness. In all my insufficiencies as a pastor, God is sufficient. Somehow, the words that need to be spoken are said, and the Lord opens hearts to receive His timely message.

Just as I did when I felt the call to ministry, Moses tried to make every excuse in the book not to follow the will of God. He held up his inadequacies and his fears to God before finally deciding to go to Egypt where he would stand in front of one of the most powerful men in the world, ask for the release of his workforce, and subsequently lead those people out of Egypt and into a foreign land. Moses had plenty to fear and an endless supply of grumblers in his ear.

After all the plagues, miracles, and wonders God performed, Pharaoh relented and allowed the Israelites out of captivity but quickly reversed his decision and sent his armies to reclaim his slaves. It is there, facing a massive sea, with Moses leading thousands of his own people, that the people began to panic at seeing Pharaoh's massive army coming. Even though they had seen the past faithfulness of God in keeping them safe from plagues and releasing them from captivity, their faith in God's power seemed to have gone missing.

Moses confidently stood in front of the Red Sea and proclaimed that they would only need to be silent, that the Lord would do the fighting. He said, "Fear not, stand firm, and see the salvation of the LORD, which he will work for you today. For the Egyptians whom you see today, you shall never see again" (v. 13).

In the same way, we must remember that the Lord will fight for us. Naturally, we will hear the armies coming, see the sea in front, and want to fight for ourselves. But could the Israelites have gotten out of captivity on their own? Could they have defeated the Egyptian army or crossed the Red Sea by their own skill or power? Neither can we secure our own salvation, manufacture a perfect peace, or overcome the anxiety of suffering.

We need only to be silent, still, and allow the Lord to do His work. We can surely rest in His might and power over our problems. It's against our nature, but it is in His will for us. Put down the weapons and lay down your defenses. The Lord will fight for you. Trust in His goodness to provide for you no matter what you face.

"Be still, and know that I am God. I will be exalted among the nations, I will be exalted in the earth!" The LORD of hosts is with us; the God of Jacob is our fortress.

—Psalm 46:10–11

DAY 29
KNOWING AND BELIEVING

"For God alone, O my soul, wait in silence, for my hope is from him. He only is my rock and my salvation, my fortress; I shall not be shaken. On God rests my salvation and my glory; my mighty rock, my refuge is God."

—Psalm 62:5–7

. . . . .

• • • • •

Theme parks are some of my least favorite places on earth. I do not do roller coasters nor do I ride any rides. I'm aware how curmudgeon this sounds, but I will be completely honest, I am scared to death of them. Too many times I have stood in the two-hour line only to bail at the last possible moment. Despite attempts and persuasions from almost everyone, I have not and will not step foot on any ride.

It seems silly to be afraid of something that is meant to be so entertaining. I can sit and watch seemingly thousands of people get on and off safely. I can even fully comprehend that I am completely safe in the harnesses, but I cannot bring myself to take the plunge. Fear keeps me on the sidelines.

There is a massive difference between knowing something and doing something. Even though my mind is certain nothing will happen, my feet will not let it happen.

As many times as we may see God's faithfulness and goodness to us in the past, and even though we may be fully aware of His trustworthiness, the most difficult task will be moving from what is in our brain to how we live in the world.

We know God is a God of peace.

We know the Lord is the Prince of Peace.

We know He calls us to run to Him when we are weary and burdened.

We know He offers us a peace that surpasses all understanding.

We know He is gracious and merciful toward us.

We know He is sovereign and in control.

Knowing all of this, how will our reactions to circumstances change? How will we react when difficulty comes? And how will it have an impact on our trust in the Lord?

As we read yesterday, the Israelites had the same problem. They saw God deliver them from captivity, part the Red Sea, bring forth water from rocks, and provide manna from heaven, yet they still had trouble faithfully obeying the will of God. They had sufficient evidence of God's faithfulness for their minds but deficient belief in their hearts to act and trust.

We must continually remind ourselves of the foundation of our faith so that when the time comes for us to exercise and rest in these truths, what we know in our minds will reach our hearts, spirit, and feet.

Knowledge of God and His nature is important, but faith in God that fuels our actions and reactions will be critical as we undergo life's trials with a sustained peace.

30 DAYS OF HOPE for PEACEFUL LIVING

DAY 30
GOD OF HOPE

"May the God of hope fill you with all joy and peace in believing, so that by the power of the Holy Spirit you may abound in hope."

—Romans 15:13

· · · · ·

• • • • •

In those first few weeks fighting through the realization of mom's grim diagnosis, we struggled with the idea of holding onto hope. The only hope we had received from doctors was the possibility that treatment would lengthen the delay of cancer's grip. But that wasn't really much hope at all. Medicine provided a sliver of hope, but the statistics always kept our expectations at bay.

The medical facts certainly did not give us what we needed. The only hope we could cling to is that death and suffering were defeated on the Cross by Christ. We could be at peace with what was happening on earth knowing what happened on the Cross to secure our salvation. Our hope mandatorily shifted from any earthly help to our heavenly hope.

We did not know how long we would enjoy my mom's presence on the earth, but we had perfect peace and hope that when it all came to an end, she would be secure in the arms of Christ. This reality served as a humbling reminder that none of us is promised tomorrow. Whether we have cancer or not, we choose today where we place our hope for tomorrow. In living in what we have been promised, we find the peace to face what is coming. We have taken the hope from our own hands and secured it in our Savior's outstretched arms. His will is not always what we want, desire, or expect, but He is faithful and trustworthy.

Although the situation was perpetually grim, God provided a miracle to us. Here are my mom's words, finishing the previously mentioned article (colorboxphotographers.com/praising-god-for-healing-update-on-jennys-cancer-journey):

So many of you have been praying along with my family and me during our dark time, and God, in His mercy, has seen fit to extend my time here on earth. I am in complete remission from the pancreatic cancer! There is no way to know how long this remission will last, but right now we are rejoicing in this amazing blessing. We thank God our Savior for this kindness.

I am humbled by God's grace and so grateful for this time extended to me. I want to thank each and every one of you who have offered prayer on our behalf and have been such an encouragement to us. You have been such a beautiful picture of the body of Christ in action. I am and will always be forever grateful.

Even still, realizing that mom is currently in complete remission from pancreatic cancer, our hope can only abound in Christ. Doctors seem puzzled at the results, and to be completely honest, we were amazed at what we were hearing.

God is faithful. God is good. He is good when there is health, and He remains good when there is cancer. He provides peace in our darkest times, and He gives hope to the hopeless. There is nowhere we can wander outside the realm of His divine goodness and no detail outside of His reign.

We have been supremely blessed by God. In the face of desperate situations, we found a God who provided a great peace that outweighed our great need.

Know that as we search for, cry out for, and hope for peace, we are desperate for something much greater. When we find God, we have found peace in His love, mercy, grace, and provision.

SCRIPTURES

Rest
Psalm 4:8
Psalm 37:39–40
Psalm 46:10–11
Psalm 116:1–9
Psalm 118:8–9

Strength
Psalm 9:9–10
Psalm 29:10–11
Psalm 46:1–3
Psalm 124:8
Ephesians 6:10–13
Colossians 1:11–14

Jesus
Isaiah 9:6–7
Matthew 5:3–12
Mark 4:35–41
John 10:14–15
John 14:1–7
John 14:25–31
Colossians 1:15-23

Suffering
Psalm 25:16–18
Philippians 3:7–11
Hebrews 12:11–14

Peace with God
Romans 5:1–5
Romans 8:5–8
Romans 8:31–39
Ephesians 2:13–22

Fear
Psalm 27:1
Psalm 34:4–8
Psalm 46:1–3
Psalm 118:5–7
2 Timothy 1:7
1 John 4:18–19

Hope
Psalm 71:12–16
Romans 12:12
Romans 15:13
2 Thessalonians 2:16–17

Rejoice
Philippians 4:4–9
1 Thessalonians 5:16–18

Miscellaneous
Matthew 5:3–12
1 Thessalonians 5:23–24
Hebrews 13:20–21
James 3:18

New Hope® Publishers is a division of WMU®, an international organization that challenges Christian believers to understand and be radically involved in God's mission. For more information about WMU, go to wmu.com. More information about New Hope books may be found at NewHopeDigital.com New Hope books may be purchased at your local bookstore.

Please go to
NewHopeDigital.com

If you've been blessed by this book,
we would like to hear your story.
The publisher and author welcome your comments and
suggestions at: newhopereader@wmu.org.